Referral-Marketing

LEGAL DISCLAIMER: This book is protected by international copyright law and may not be copied, reproduced, given away, or used to create derivative works without the publisher's expressed permission. The publisher retains full copyrights to this book.

The author has made every reasonable effort to be as accurate and complete as possible in the creation of this book and to ensure that the information provided is free from errors; however, the author/publisher/ reseller assumes no responsibility for errors, omissions, or contrary interpretation of the subject matter herein and does not warrant or represent at any time that the contents within are accurate due to the rapidly changing nature of the Internet.

Any perceived slights of specific persons, peoples, or organizations are unintentional.

The purpose of this book is to educate and there are no guarantees of income, sales or results implied. The publisher/author/reseller can therefore not be held accountable for any poor results you may attain when implementing the techniques or when following any guidelines set out for you in this book.

Any product, website, and company names mentioned in this report are the trademarks or copyright properties of their respective owners. The author/publisher/reseller are not associated or affiliated with them in any way. Nor does the referred product, website, and company names sponsor, endorse, or approve this product.

Table of Contents

Table of Contents 3

Introduction 5

Become Share-Worthy 8

Network with Influencers 13

Timing is Everything 16

Tweak Your Referral Sign Up Page 23

Always Follow Up 25

Be Innovative 27

Offer Additional Incentives 29

Join Perkzilla 31

Final Words 33

Resources 35

Introduction

If you're looking to maximize exposure and profits while consistently working towards acquiring new customers, there is no better way than with referral marketing.

Referral marketing is all about encouraging people in your niche to share your products and services. This can include customers, influencers and thought leaders in your market.

Ultimately, there is no easier way to better position your brand and leverage your existing customer base than to design a referral system that actively encourages sharing.

There are many ways to create a referral system for your business. You could choose to compensate referrals based on a specific cash value, credit towards purchases made on your shop, or other incentive-based offers that motivate people to share your products and services amongst their own inner circles.

The problem is, many people don't spend enough time analyzing what is currently working in their market so they can design a referral program around what is likely to move the needle.

Worse, many businesses overlook referral marketing altogether and do little more than set up a basic affiliate program and hope it will help them expand their outreach.

Build it and they will come simply doesn't work when it comes to creating a successful referral program. The key is to analyze your market so that your platform will attract the **right** customers.

While a basic affiliate program is a great asset to your business and can help elevate your platform and broaden your outreach, it's only the beginning. There are many other ways to utilize the power of referral marketing and that's what this special report is all about.

I'll show you how to connect with your most loyal customers so you can motivate them to spread the word about your business, while setting yourself up for long-term success.

Are you ready to maximize your profits and level-up your game with referral marketing?

Let's begin!

Become Share-Worthy

When it comes to taking advantage of the power of referral marketing, it all begins with ensuring your business is share-worthy.

The goal is to persuade existing customers, thought leaders and influencers to promote your products and recommend them to others. So, the better you structure your business to appeal to your target audience, and the more excited you get people, the easier it will be to launch your referral program.

Think about it: if your products and services don't include a clear brand message that tells a potential customer exactly how they benefit from purchasing from you, chances are your affiliates will have to do way too much work to get the sale.

Remember, it's not their job to persuade a prospect into making a purchase – **it's yours.**

The key is to get your customers excited about your message so that they are motivated to spread the word. You can do this several ways, including through monetized campaigns (affiliate programs, rewards or other incentives), and of course, by creating a product that stands out in the market, is in-demand, and solves a specific problem.

Regardless of your strategy, you need to make sure that you focus on highlighting the benefits of your product or service. You'll want to spend time working on a killer sales page while fine-tuning your shop or business landing page so that it offers a positive user experience.

Simplicity is key! You want potential customers to land on your page and get excited about what you have to offer. At the same time, your referral program should follow this same format.

And above all else, making sure that your customers are happy and that they feel you are a quality provider is essential in generating new business and persuading others that you're worth recommending to their friends, family or colleagues.

Focus on over-delivering and exceeding expectations!

According to recent surveys and statistics, 62% of people do a thorough internet search before buying a product. They want to see what actual customers have to say about a company before handing over their money.

In addition to reading ratings and reviews, 90% of buyers rely on brand recommendations from people they know. Just think about the last time you made a big-ticket purchase. You probably asked around to see what people recommended, right?

At the very least, you likely spent some time reading through reviews and feedback left by people who had already purchased the product you're considering. So, it's important to make sure that if someone searches for your product or service, all they see are glowing testimonials and positive feedback. You do this by over-delivering and providing the best user experience possible.

With every customer transaction, you want to encourage them to share your product with others, either directly or indirectly through their social media platforms and outreach.

Here are a few ways to get started:

- Customers always appreciate a discount, or you can even give them a gift just for providing their feedback.

- For those who are more interested in boosting their internet clout, offer to do a shout-out to their social media page in return for a testimonial or share.

- A testimonial-style video created by satisfied customers can become instrumental in convincing new customers to take a chance on your products or services.

- Take time to share positive feedback you receive on both your business website and social media accounts. Give potential customers as much opportunity as possible to see how customers are responding to your services.

Word of mouth might be the most important part of your marketing since 75% of people have little faith in traditional advertisements. Genuine endorsements from people they know or respect will go the distance.

After each transaction, find a polite and non-intrusive way to ask customers to tell their friends and family about their buying experience. On average, people are four times more likely to do business with you if they were referred by a friend!

Network with Influencers

Social media influencers and thought leaders are, without a doubt, incredibly valuable partners when it comes to helping you reach new customers.

Influencers are people on social media with a strong following. Their followers rely on them for advice on what products they should and shouldn't buy. Many of these influencers do this as a full-time job.

Social media influencers tend to be very active on their pages, and reach out to their followers on a regular basis. Usually they use one of the following platforms to communicate:

1. Instagram
2. SnapChat
3. YouTube
4. Twitter

5. Facebook

In order to get these influencers to try your product and share their experience with their followers, consider sending them a free sample of your product.

Sampling is especially popular in the beauty industry, where influencers often record themselves unboxing a product or trying a product they received and then giving an honest review.

According to statistics, 40% of people purchased a product after watching an influencer on social media who endorsed the product. Another statistic shows that 49% of buyers strictly rely on suggestions from influencers.

That's nearly half of all consumers!

If you haven't done so already, designate a budget strictly for influencer marketing.

If you have long-term, repeat customers, go out of your way to show your appreciation. People who stick with a company for a long period of time want to feel acknowledged and appreciated.

You should make a habit of reviewing and discussing any negative feedback you receive as well. Look at this as important feedback that will help you improve your products or services.

Don't focus just on the positive comments and reviews you receive! If you want to take your business to the next level, you need to be diligent in reviewing the 5-star reviews right down to the 1-star reviews so you can improve on weaknesses in your business.

Timing is Everything

Customers are most likely to share their experiences immediately after they have made a purchase if they are directly asked to do so. Their adrenaline is high and they're usually excited, which is the perfect time to introduce your referral program to them.

Not only is this a great time to give them the opportunity to become an affiliate, but it's often a good time to ask for feedback on their overall buying experience.

Note that a customer who just purchased a product won't be able to provide feedback about that product, however they will be able to provide information about their overall buying experience.

Are you encouraging reviews and feedback for your product that you can then use as social proof for your sales pages and referral program?

You might be surprised to know how often businesses fail to reach out and ask for feedback from existing customers. Don't be one of those people!

By connecting to your customers and asking them for information about their experiences using your product, you'll be able to generate testimonials that you can use within your marketing campaigns. So, don't be afraid to ask!

Quite often, you'll be able to win someone over just by reaching out and asking for their feedback. This makes them feel important and demonstrates that you value them as a customer and that you're committed to ensuring they have a positive interaction and buying experience.

When it comes to collecting this information, you can use automation tools to cut down your workload and streamline the process.

Here are a few ideas:

Use Surveys

Create a survey that asks for pertinent information associated with their buying experience. Keep the survey simple, short and focused. Don't bog customers down by requiring that they complete multiple pages to get through the process.

Focus only on the questions that are most important in helping you identify potential issues and improve your products and services.

Use Autoresponders

Hopefully you've already incorporated a newsletter or mailing list into your sales system so that you're collecting customers' information and following up with them.

You can extend the value of your mailing list by loading autoresponders with a sequence of emails that work towards building relationships with your customers.

At some point during this sequence, you can set an email to go out that asks for feedback. You'll likely want to incorporate this somewhat early in the sequence, but not the initial email.

Give your customer some time to use your product or service so that they can provide in-depth feedback and insight that will help you improve their experience.

Incorporate an Affiliate Program

Introduce and inform existing customers about the benefits of your referral program, such as receiving a discount on their next purchase and of course, earning money from sales generated because of their marketing.

Have you ever heard of the Net Promoter Score (NPS)?

It's a ranking system built on surveys. The higher your NPS score, the more likely you are to attract new customers through referral marketing because it ultimately helps you gauge the loyalty of your customer base.

You can find out more here:

https://www.checkmarket.com/blog/net-promoter-score/

When you're ready to start calculating your NPS, you can build your own survey simply by using a tool like Survey Monkey.

The key is to simply ask them, "On a scale of 1-10, how likely are you to recommend our services to friends or family?"

You can then categorize responses according to the level in which they are likely to refer your business to others. With NPS, a score of 0-6 is considered detractors, 7-8 are passives and 9-10 are promotors.

A great way to use the power of NPS is to take things one step further. After someone completes your survey, you can segment responses so that those who submitted a score of 7+ are then redirected to your affiliate program where they are given an invitation to sign up to promote your products.

You can also have customer service representatives promote your referral program at the end of positive phone calls.

When you initially rollout your referral program, it's important to notify your most loyal customers first. These are the people who would appreciate a reward for their loyalty, and they'll be more likely to refer you to friends and family when there's money to be saved.

In addition to the above ways you can educate customers on your referral program, make sure that you regularly remind them about it. Reminders can come in the form of emails, the bottom of receipts, and links and ads on your website.

Tweak Your Referral Sign Up Page

First, you'll want to make sure that you are transparent about the terms of your referral program and all that it offers. There are a lot of scams out there, so customers are justifiably cautious when it comes to taking part in a referral program.

After all, they are spending their time promoting you and risking their reputation when recommending your products and services.

This means your sign-up page should be very clear and easy to understand, leaving no room for misunderstandings.

Here are a few things to keep in mind:

- Outline the rules and terms of your referral program.

- Highlight the benefits of joining your referral program.

- Provide clear instructions and information on when payment is remitted and how.

- Choose a reward carefully that aligns with your market and what they will be most interested in.

- Simple eligibility criteria. You don't want to complicate the sign-up process.

You want to keep the details about your referral program as simple as possible. For example, a referrer gets A for every lead and B for the first sale.

Always Follow Up

Good customer service is at the heart of every successful company. Whether it's on the phone, online, or via a text message, customers want to be taken care of. As a business that wants them to refer new customers, you want to provide them with good support.

One of the most important parts of quality customer service is to be responsive. If a customer files a complaint, they want to hear back from you immediately. Many of them now use social media instead of calling a company, too.

For example, an upset customer might reach out to your Twitter account to complain. All it takes is a few seconds to reply.

Stay on top of all social media comments from customers, and make complaints your number one concern. Customers understand that stuff happens, and they're more likely to refer you if they know you take issues seriously and handle them promptly.

Encourage your customer service representatives to be sincere when dealing with every client. Make sure they maintain a clear, professional tone, and are never too pushy.

On top of manual customer service attention, look into having a customer ticketing software system. This system allows each complaint to go through a thorough process to ensure every single one is taken care of.

Above all else, remember that people will almost always remember how you made them feel, so aim for a happy ending to all issues reported.

Be Innovative

Even if your business is doing well, there's always room to grow. You can drastically improve the number of referrals your company receives simply by being innovative and offering something new – something your market is missing.

Remember, there's almost always a way to make a product or service faster and better.

Developing a new product doesn't have to be as big as making a new kind of phone or car, though. Innovation is all about meeting a need with a service.

Pay attention to the needs of, not just your customers, but consumers in general. What are some products and services that people are requesting? What complaints do they have about current products?

Meet those needs and customers will refer new clients to your business.

Offer Additional Incentives

One great way to jump-start your referral marketing is to offer existing customers with additional discounts and rewards at the time of purchase.

For example, consider offering a coupon code or special discount in exchange for that customer sharing their purchase with his/her friends via social media.

Groupon did this very well by offering large discounts for every referral a person made via social media. Providing discount and savings options is a fantastic way to not only encourage referrals, but to reward existing customers by making their purchase more affordable.

It's a win-win!

Study your market to determine what type of discount or other financial incentive they would be most interested in.

- Are they looking for a coupon code on a certain product?
- Would they prefer a discount on their current order or a future purchase?
- Would they like a percentage off an entire order rather than a discount on just one product?

Test out different incentive offers to see what your market will best respond to. Remember to always keep track of your incentive campaigns so you can adequately measure results.

Join Perkzilla

If you really want to get people talking about your business, then you should consider joining Perkzilla, the Referral Marketing Monster at https://www.PerkZilla.com

Perkzilla makes it easy for your your business will stand out in a crowded marketplace by helping you create viral marketing campaigns that will quickly maximize your business's exposure.

The company's proven strategies, when implemented with your website, will help you build client lists, increase traffic, and significantly grow your business.

Perkzilla will also teach you all about the psychological triggers that are guaranteed to get people talking about your company. The more customers talk about their positive experiences with your company, the more likely you are to get referrals.

One of the best parts about Perkzilla is that you can do all of this without the use of paid ads. Word of mouth referrals are completely free, and Perkzilla will help you get more business this way without having to spend money on paid advertisements.

PerkZilla also effortlessly integrates with various autoresponder services and mailing list providers.

Final Words

Maximizing exposure and reaching new customers is easy with referral marketing. It begins by creating a referral program that clearly outlines your terms, requirements, payment options and benefits.

Then, make sure to deliver any incentives immediately, or if offering cash rewards, set up a delivery schedule that your referrals understand and stick to it.

Make sure to promote your referral program everywhere possible, including via social media, your website, newsletter, in purchase receipts and in follow-up emails.

Don't be afraid to ask existing customers to join your referral program. Happy customers who continue to purchase from you often make the best affiliates because they know your products and have personal experience with your business.

Make sure to reach out personally to your top affiliates. Provide additional compensation or rewards to those who work hard to acquire new customers on your behalf. People appreciate receiving tokens of appreciation even if it's a simple thank you note.

I hope this report has provided you with the information you need to create a successful referral program of your own.

To your success,

Resources

Here are links to a few resources that I believe will help you:

How to Encourage Customer Referrals:

>>https://www.buyapowa.com/blog/10-tips-encourage-customer-referrals/

Increasing Referrals:

>>https://www.campaignmonitor.com/blog/email-marketing/2018/01/7-marketing-strategies-increase-referrals/

Tips on Referral Marketing:

>>https://www.oberlo.com/blog/referral-marketing

Made in the USA
Las Vegas, NV
26 December 2023